THE 30-MINUTE SHAKESPEARE
MUCH ADO ABOUT NOTHING

✳

"Nick Newlin's work as a teaching artist for Folger Education during the past thirteen years has provided students, regardless of their experience with Shakespeare or being on stage, a unique opportunity to tread the boards at the Folger Theatre. Working with students to edit Shakespeare's plays for performance at the annual Folger Shakespeare Festivals has enabled students to gain new insights into the Bard's plays, build their skills of comprehension and critical reading, and just plain have fun working collaboratively with their peers.

Folger Education promotes performance-based teaching of Shakespeare's plays, providing students with an interactive approach to Shakespeare's plays in which they participate in a close reading of the text through intellectual, physical, and vocal engagement. Newlin's *The 30-Minute Shakespeare* series is an invaluable resource for teachers of Shakespeare, and for all who are interested in performing the plays."

ROBERT YOUNG, PH.D.
DIRECTOR OF EDUCATION
FOLGER SHAKESPEARE LIBRARY

Much Ado About Nothing: The 30-Minute Shakespeare
ISBN 978-1-935550-03-7
Adaptation, essays, and notes © 2010 by Nick Newlin

Cover design by Sarah Juckniess
Printed in the United States of America

Distributed by Consortium Book Sales & Distribution
www.cbsd.com

NICOLO WHIMSEY PRESS
www.30MinuteShakespeare.com

Art Director: Sarah Juckniess
Managing Editor: Katherine Little

MUCH ADO ABOUT NOTHING

THE 30-MINUTE SHAKESPEARE

Written by WILLIAM SHAKESPEARE

Abridged AND Edited
by NICK NEWLIN

Nicolo Whimsey
Press

Brandywine, MD

To my Dad,
Bill Newlin—
a wonderful
role model

Special thanks to Joanne Flynn, Bill Newlin, Eliza Newlin Carney, William and Louisa Newlin, Michael Tolaydo, Hilary Kacser, Sarah Juckniess, Katherine Little, Eva Zimmerman, Julie Schaper and all of Consortium, Leo Bowman and the students, faculty, and staff at Banneker Academic High School, and Robert Young Ph.D., and the Folger Shakespeare Library, especially the wonderful Education Department.

✳ TABLE OF CONTENTS

✳ NO EXPERIENCE NECESSARY

I was not a big "actor type" in high school, so if you weren't either, or if the young people you work with are not, then this book is for you. Whether or not you work with "actor types," you can use this book to stage a lively and captivating thirty-minute version of a Shakespeare play. No experience is necessary.

When I was about eleven years old, my parents took me to see Shakespeare's *Two Gentlemen of Verona*, which was being performed as a Broadway musical. I didn't comprehend every word I heard, but I was enthralled with the language, the characters, and the story, and I understood enough of it to follow along. From then on, I associated Shakespeare with *fun*.

Of course Shakespeare is fun. The Elizabethan audiences knew it, which is one reason he was so popular. It didn't matter that some of the language eluded them. The characters were passionate and vibrant, and their conflicts were compelling. Young people study Shakespeare in high school, but more often than not they read his work like a text book and then get quizzed on academic elements of the play, such as plot, theme, and vocabulary. These are all very interesting, but not nearly as interesting as standing up and performing a scene! It is through performance that the play comes alive and all its "academic" elements are revealed. There is nothing more satisfying to a student or teacher than the feeling of "owning" a Shakespeare play, and that can only come from performing it.

But Shakespeare's plays are often two or more hours long, making the performance of an entire play almost out of the question. One can perform a single scene, which is certainly a good start, but what about the story? What about the changes a character goes through as the play progresses? When school groups perform one scene unedited, or when they lump several plays together, the audience can get lost. This is why I have always preferred to tell the story of the play.

The 30-Minute Shakespeare gives students and teachers a chance to get up on their feet and act out a Shakespeare play in half an hour, using his language. The emphasis is on key scenes, with narrative bridges between scenes to keep the audience caught up on the action. The stage directions are built into this script so that young actors do not have to stand in one place; they can move and tell the story with their actions as well as their words. And it can all be done in a classroom during class time!

That is where this book was born: not in a research library, a graduate school lecture, a professional stage, or even an after-school drama club. All of the play cuttings in *The 30-Minute Shakespeare* were first rehearsed in a D.C. public high school English class, and performed successfully at the Folger Shakespeare Library's annual Secondary School Shakespeare Festival. The players were not necessarily "actor types." For many of them, this was their first performance in a play.

Something almost miraculous happens when students perform Shakespeare. They "get" it. By occupying the characters and speaking the words out loud, students gain a level of understanding and appreciation that is unachievable by simply reading the text. That is the magic of a performance-based method of learning Shakespeare, and this book makes the formerly daunting task of staging a Shakespeare play possible for anybody.

With *The 30-Minute Shakespeare* book series I hope to help teachers and students produce a Shakespeare play in a short amount of time, thus jump-starting the process of discovering the beauty, magic, and fun of the Bard. Plot, theme, and language reveal themselves through the performance of these half-hour play cuttings, and everybody involved receives the priceless gift of "owning" a piece of Shakespeare. The result is an experience that is fun and engaging, and one that we can all carry with us as we play out our own lives on the stages of the world.

NICK NEWLIN
Brandywine, MD
March 2010

CHARACTERS IN THE PLAY

The following is a list of characters that appear in this cutting of Much Ado About Nothing.

Fourteen actors performed in the original production. This number can be increased to about thirty or decreased to about twelve by having actors share or double roles.

For the full breakdown of characters, see Sample Program.

BEATRICE: Leonato's niece and Hero's cousin

BENEDICK: A young lord of Padua

DON PEDRO: Prince of Aragon

BALTHASAR: Attendant on Don Pedro

DON JUAN: Don Pedro's illegitimate brother

LEONATO: Governor of Messina

CLAUDIO: A young lord of Florence

HERO: Leonato's daughter

MARGARET:
URSULA: } Gentlewomen attending on Hero

FRIAR FRANCIS: A priest

DOGBERRY: Master constable

VERGES: Dogberry's assistant.

NARRATORS

✳ SCENE 1. (ACT I, SCENE I)

Before Leonato's house.

STAGEHANDS ONE AND TWO *set bench downstage left, slightly angled up toward center.* **STAGEHANDS THREE AND FOUR** *bring on plant and set downstage, left of bench.*

NARRATOR *enters from rear curtain and comes downstage center.*

> As the war ends, the soldiers return to Messina where they are warmly greeted by the Governor, Leonato. Benedick and Beatrice renew their battle of wits.

Exit **NARRATOR** *stage right.*

Enter **LEONATO, HERO,** *and* **BEATRICE,** *with* **BALTHASAR,** *from stage left.*

BEATRICE
> I pray you, is Signior Benedick returned from the wars or no?

BALTHASAR
> O, he's returned; and as pleasant as ever he was.

BEATRICE
> I pray you, how many hath he killed and eaten in these wars?

LEONATO

> Faith, niece, you tax Signior Benedick too much;
> but he'll be meet with you, I doubt it not.

BALTHASAR

> He hath done good service, lady, in these wars.

BEATRICE

> He hath an excellent stomach.
> He is no less than a stuffed man:
> but for the stuffing,—well, we are all mortal.

LEONATO

> You must not, sir, mistake my niece. There is a kind
> of merry war betwixt Signior Benedick and her:
> they never meet but there's a skirmish of wit
> between them.

BEATRICE

> In our last conflict four of his five wits went halting
> off, and now is the whole man governed with one.

BALTHASAR

> Don Pedro is approached.

Enter DON PEDRO, DON JOHN, CLAUDIO, *and* BENEDICK *from stage right. All on stage move stage left.* DON PEDRO *and* LEONATO *stand center,* CLAUDIO *and* BENEDICK *to the right.* DON JOHN *stands to the far right, a little removed from the group.*

DON PEDRO

> Good Signior Leonato, you are come to meet your
> trouble: the fashion of the world is to avoid cost, and
> you encounter it.

LEONATO

> Never came trouble to my house in the likeness of
> your grace: for trouble being gone, comfort should
> remain; but when you depart from me, sorrow
> abides and happiness takes his leave.

BENEDICK *(moves left toward* **BEATRICE***; she sits on the bench as*
he continues to stand)

> What, my dear Lady Disdain! are you yet living?

BEATRICE

> Is it possible disdain should die while she hath such
> meet food to feed it as Signior Benedick? Courtesy
> itself must convert to disdain, if you come in her
> presence.

BENEDICK

> Then is courtesy a turncoat. But it is certain I am
> loved of all ladies, only you excepted: and I would I
> could find in my heart that I had not a hard heart; for,
> truly, I love none. *(sits next to* **BEATRICE***; she stands)*

BEATRICE

> A dear happiness to women: they would else have
> been troubled with a pernicious suitor. I thank God
> and my cold blood, I am of your humour for that: I
> had rather hear my dog bark at a crow than a man
> swear he loves me.

BENEDICK

> Well, you are a rare parrot-teacher. *(steps one step*
> *closer to her)*

BEATRICE

> A bird of my tongue is better than a beast of yours.
> *(steps one step closer to him)*

BENEDICK

> I would my horse had the speed of your tongue,
> and so good a continuer. But keep your way, i' God's
> name; I have done. *(turns his back and sits facing*
> *away from her)*

BEATRICE

> You always end with a jade's trick: I know you of old.
> *(turns her back and sits facing away from him)*

LEONATO *(to* DON JOHN*)*

> Let me bid you welcome, my lord: being reconciled
> to the prince your brother, I owe you all duty.

DON JOHN

> I thank you: I am not of many words, but I thank you.

LEONATO *(to* DON PEDRO*)*

> Please it your grace lead on?

DON PEDRO

> Your hand, Leonato; we will go together.

Exeunt all stage right.

✳ SCENE 2. (ACT II, SCENE III)

Leonato's orchard.

NARRATOR *enters from rear curtain and walks downstage center.*

> Benedick declares that he will never love one
> woman; The three men trick Benedick into believing
> Beatrice loves him. Benedick falls for it and decides
> to love Beatrice.

Exit **NARRATOR** *stage left.*

Enter **BENEDICK** *from stage right and walks downstage center.*

BENEDICK

> Love may transform me to an oyster; but I'll take my
> oath on it, till he have made an oyster of me, he shall
> never make me a fool. One woman is fair, yet I am
> well; another is wise, yet I am well; another virtuous,
> yet I am well; but till all graces be in one woman,
> one woman shall not come in my grace
> Ha! the prince and Monsieur Love! I will hide me in
> the arbour. *(hides behind stage left pillar)*

Enter **DON PEDRO, CLAUDIO,** *and* **LEONATO.** *They stand downstage center.*

DON PEDRO

> See you where Benedick hath hid himself?
> *(louder, so that* **BENEDICK** *hears)*
> Come hither, Leonato. What was it you told me of

to-day, that your niece Beatrice was in love with
Signior Benedick?

BENEDICK *hides behind plant and starts to inch toward the
others, until plant is to the right of the bench.*

CLAUDIO

I did never think that lady would have loved any
man.

LEONATO

No, nor I neither; but most wonderful that she
should so dote on Signior Benedick, whom she hath
in all outward behaviors seemed ever to abhor.

BENEDICK *(pops his head up from behind plant)*
Is't possible? Sits the wind in that corner?

DON PEDRO

Why, what effects of passion shows she?

CLAUDIO

Bait the hook well; this fish will bite.

CLAUDIO *starts to walk left, in front of plant and bench, and the
others follow.* DON PEDRO, LEONATO, *and* CLAUDIO *all sit on bench.*

DON PEDRO

How, how, pray you? You amaze me: I would have
I thought her spirit had been invincible against all
assaults of affection.

LEONATO

I would have sworn it had, my lord; especially
against Benedick.

BENEDICK *(from behind plant, head popping up)*
I should think this a gull, but that the white-bearded
fellow speaks it: knavery cannot, sure, hide himself
in such reverence. *(sees others looking toward him
and pops his head back down quickly)*

CLAUDIO
He hath ta'en the infection: hold it up.

*The three men stand up and start walking stage right, in front of
pillar, just to bother* **BENEDICK** *and make him follow so that he
can listen.*

DON PEDRO
Hath she made her affection known to Benedick?

LEONATO
No; and swears she never will: that's her torment.

BENEDICK, *frustrated at not being able to hear, starts crawling
out from behind plant and tries to get behind stage right pillar.*

LEONATO
She'll be up twenty times a night, and there will she
sit in her smock till she have writ a sheet of paper:
my daughter tells us all.

CLAUDIO
Now you talk of a sheet of paper, I remember a
pretty jest your daughter told us of.

LEONATO
O, when she had writ it and was reading it over, she
found Benedick and Beatrice between the sheet?

BENEDICK *stops midcrawl. Others look over, so* **BENEDICK,** *center
stage, pretends he is a bench.*

LEONATO

> O, she tore the letter into a thousand halfpence;
> railed at herself, that she should be so immodest to
> write to one that she knew would flout her;

CLAUDIO

> Then down upon her knees she falls, weeps, sobs,
> beats her heart, tears her hair, prays, curses; "O sweet
> Benedick! God give me patience!"

CLAUDIO *walks over to* BENEDICK *(still as a bench) and sits on his back.* BENEDICK *reacts to strain with facial expressions, etc.*

DON PEDRO

> It were good that Benedick knew of it by some other,
> if she will not discover it.

DON PEDRO *also sits on* BENEDICK, *who reacts to the increased strain.*

CLAUDIO

> To what end? He would make but a sport of it and
> torment the poor lady worse.

DON PEDRO

> If she should make tender of her love, 'tis very
> possible he'll scorn it; for the man, as you know all,
> hath a contemptible spirit. I am sorry for your niece.
> Shall we go seek Benedick, and tell him of her love?

CLAUDIO

> Never tell him, my lord: let her wear it out with good
> counsel.

LEONATO

> Nay, that's impossible: she may wear her heart out first.

LEONATO *sits on* BENEDICK *as well.* BENEDICK *is about to lose it and can barely hold them.*

DON PEDRO
> Well, we will hear further of it by your daughter: let it cool the while. I love Benedick well; and I could wish he would modestly examine himself, to see how much he is unworthy so good a lady.

LEONATO
> My lord, will you walk? dinner is ready.

DON PEDRO
> Let there be the same net spread for her.

Exit DON PEDRO, CLAUDIO, *and* LEONATO *stage right.*

BENEDICK *(coming forward, dealing with his aching back)*
> This can be no trick: They have the truth of this from Hero. They seem to pity the lady: it seems her affections have their full bent. Love me! why, it must be requited. I hear how I am censured: I did never think to marry: I must not seem proud: They say the lady is fair; 'tis a truth; and wise, but for loving me; I will be horribly in love with her. The world must be peopled. When I said I would die a bachelor, I did not think I should live till I were married.

Exit BENEDICK *stage right.*

✳ **SCENE 3.** (ACT III, SCENE I)

Leonato's garden.

NARRATOR *enters from rear curtain and walks downstage center.*

>Now it is the women's turn to trick Beatrice into believing that Benedick loves her. She falls for it and decides to love Benedick. Where is this all leading?

Exit **NARRATOR** *stage left.*

Enter **HERO, MARGARET,** *and* **URSULA** *from stage right. They walk to stage left bench and sit.*

HERO

>Now, Ursula, Margaret, when Beatrice doth come,
>My talk to thee must be how Benedick
>Is sick in love with Beatrice.

Enter **BEATRICE,** *from behind rear curtain. She hides behind stage left pillar.*

>Now begin.

URSULA

>But are you sure
>That Benedick loves Beatrice so entirely?

HERO

>So says the prince and my new-trothed lord.

MARGARET

And did they bid you tell her of it, madam?

HERO

They did entreat me to acquaint her of it;
But I persuaded them, if they loved Benedick,
To wish him wrestle with affection,
And never to let Beatrice know of it.

BEATRICE *moves from behind stage right pillar, and hides behind plant, which is to right of bench.*

URSULA

Why did you so? Doth not the gentleman
Deserve as full as fortunate a bed
As ever Beatrice shall couch upon?

HERO

She is so self-endeared.

All three women look at **BEATRICE**, *who freezes with her arms out like a plant's branches. During* **MARGARET'S** *speech,* **BEATRICE** *slowly rises from behind the plant.*

MARGARET

Sure, I think so;
And therefore certainly it were not good
She knew his love, lest she make sport at it.

MARGARET *looks at* **BEATRICE**, *who freezes with her arms out again.*

URSULA

Such carping is not commendable.

HERO

But who dare tell her so? If I should speak,
She would mock me into air;

MARGARET

> She's limed, I warrant you: we have caught her, madam.

HERO

> If it proves so, then loving goes by haps:
> Some Cupid kills with arrows, some with traps.

Exit HERO, MARGARET, *and* URSULA *stage left.*

BEATRICE *(coming forward)*

> What fire is in mine ears? Can this be true?
> Stand I condemn'd for pride and scorn so much?
> Contempt, farewell! and maiden pride, adieu!
> No glory lives behind the back of such.
> And, Benedick, love on; I will requite thee,
> Taming my wild heart to thy loving hand:
> If thou dost love, my kindness shall incite thee
> To bind our loves up in a holy band;
> For others say thou dost deserve, and I
> Believe it better than reportingly.

Exit BEATRICE *stage right.*

STAGEHANDS ONE AND TWO *remove bench.* STAGEHANDS THREE
AND FOUR *remove plant.*

✳ SCENE 4. (ACT IV, SCENE I)

A church.

NARRATOR *enters from rear curtain and walks downstage center.*

> At the wedding of Claudio and Hero, Claudio, having been tricked into believing Hero has been unfaithful, refuses to marry her. Friar Francis hatches a scheme to right this wrong.

Exit **NARRATOR** *stage left.*

SOUND OPERATOR *plays* Sound Cue #1 *("Wedding March").*

Enter **FRIAR FRANCIS, LEONATO, HERO,** *and* **BEATRICE** *from stage right,* **DON PEDRO, CLAUDIO, BENEDICK,** *and* **DON JOHN** *from stage left.*

FRIAR FRANCIS *(to* CLAUDIO*)*
> You come hither, my lord, to marry this lady.

CLAUDIO *(long pause, staring straight ahead with no eye contact)*
> No.

Everyone looks at **CLAUDIO.** *Some think he is joking and laugh just a little, while others are confused. The soldiers are serious.*

LEONATO *(trying to half-laugh and keep things light)*
> To be married to her: friar, you come to marry her.

FRIAR FRANCIS
> Lady, you come hither to be married to this count.

HERO
> I do.

FRIAR FRANCIS
> If either of you know any inward impediment why
> you should not be conjoined, charge you, on your
> souls, to utter it.

CLAUDIO
> Know you any, Hero?

HERO
> None, my lord.

FRIAR FRANCIS
> Know you any, count?

LEONATO
> I dare make his answer, none.

CLAUDIO
> O, what men dare do! what men may do! what men
> daily do, not knowing what they do!
> Stand thee by, friar.

FRIAR FRANCIS *moves out of the way, to stage right.*

> Father, by your leave:
> Will you with free and unconstrained soul
> Give me this maid, your daughter?

LEONATO
> As freely, son, as God did give her me.

CLAUDIO

There, Leonato, take her back again:

He grabs HERO *by the shoulders and shoves her back to* LEONATO. *The others gasp.* LEONATO *holds* HERO, *comforting her, and* BEATRICE *comes to her side too.*

(to LEONATO*)* Give not this rotten orange to your
friend;
She's but the sign and semblance of her honour.
Behold how like a maid she blushes here!
But she is none:
She knows the heat of a luxurious bed; *(*HERO *gasps
audibly)*
Her blush is guiltiness, not modesty.

LEONATO

What do you mean, my lord?

CLAUDIO

Not to be married,
Not to knit my soul to an approved wanton.
(turning toward HERO*)* You seem to me as Dian in
her orb,
(sincere and sorrowful) As chaste as is the bud ere it
be blown;
(now angry) But you are more intemperate in your
blood
Than Venus, or those pamper'd animals
That rage in savage sensuality.

LEONATO *starts to come at* CLAUDIO *as if he's going to swing at him;* BEATRICE *and* FRIAR FRANCIS *hold him back.*

DON JOHN

Sir, they are spoken, and these things are true.

BENEDICK *(aside to audience)*
> This looks not like a nuptial.

HERO
> True! O God!

CLAUDIO
> Is this face Hero's? Are our eyes our own?

HERO
> O, God defend me! how am I beset!

CLAUDIO
> To make you answer truly to your name.

HERO
> Is it not Hero? Who can blot that name?

CLAUDIO
> Marry, that can Hero;
> Hero itself can blot out Hero's virtue.
> What man was he talk'd with you yesternight
> Out at your window betwixt twelve and one?
> Now, if you are a maid, answer to this.

HERO
> I talk'd with no man at that hour, my lord.

DON PEDRO
> Why, then are you no maiden. Leonato,
> I am sorry you must hear: upon mine honour,
> Myself, my brother and this grieved count
> Did see her, hear her, at that hour last night
> Talk with a ruffian at her chamber-window
> Who hath indeed, most like a liberal villain,

Confess'd the vile encounters they have had
A thousand times in secret.

DON JOHN

Fie, fie! they are not to be named, my lord,
Not to be spoke of. Thus, pretty lady,
I am sorry for thy much misgovernment.

CLAUDIO

O Hero, what a Hero hadst thou been,
If half thy outward graces had been placed
About thy thoughts and counsels of thy heart!
But fare thee well, most foul, most fair! farewell,
Thou pure impiety and impious purity!
For thee I'll lock up all the gates of love,
And on my eyelids shall conjecture hang,
To turn all beauty into thoughts of harm,
And never shall it more be gracious. *(turns his back
to* HERO*)*

LEONATO

Hath no man's dagger here a point for me?

HERO *swoons;* BEATRICE *helps catch her and bends down to
comfort her.*

BEATRICE

Why, how now, cousin! wherefore sink you down?

DON JOHN

Come, let us go.

Exit DON PEDRO, DON JOHN, *and* CLAUDIO *stage left.*

LEONATO *(standing above* BEATRICE, *pointing)*

Do not live, Hero; do not ope thine eyes:

(*walks downstage center, looking out to audience*)
Why ever wast thou lovely in my eyes?
(*with sadness*) Mine and mine I loved and mine I praised
And mine that I was proud on, mine so much
That I myself was to myself not mine,
Valuing of her,—why, she,
(*now angrily*) O, she is fallen
Into a pit of ink, that the wide sea
Hath drops too few to wash her clean again.

FRIAR FRANCIS (*coming downstage toward* **LEONATO**)
Hear me a little;
By noting of the lady I have mark'd
A thousand blushing apparitions
To start into her face, a thousand innocent shames
In angel whiteness beat away those blushes;
Trust not my age,
My reverence, calling, nor divinity,
If this sweet lady lie not guiltless here
Under some biting error.

HERO (*pleading, on her knees*)
O my father,
Prove you that I yesternight
Maintain'd the change of words with any creature,
Refuse me, hate me, torture me to death!

FRIAR FRANCIS
There is some strange misprision in the princes.

BENEDICK
Two of them have the very bent of honour;
And if their wisdoms be misled in this,
The practise of it lives in John the bastard,
Whose spirits toil in frame of villanies.

LEONATO

I know not.
(threateningly) If they wrong her honour,
The proudest of them shall well hear of it.

FRIAR FRANCIS

Pause awhile, *(looks around, as if telling a secret, but
still loud enough for audience to hear)*
Your daughter here the princes left for dead:
Let her awhile be secretly kept in,
And publish it that she is dead indeed
and do all rites that appertain unto a burial.

LEONATO

What shall become of this? what will this do?

FRIAR FRANCIS

This shall on her behalf
Change slander to remorse;
So will it fare with Claudio:
When he shall hear she died upon his words,
The idea of her life shall sweetly creep
Into his study of imagination,
(optimistic and comforting) Come, lady, die to live:
this wedding-day
Perhaps is but prolong'd: have patience and endure.

Exit all but **BENEDICK** *and* **BEATRICE,** *who has moved stage left,
leaning on pillar, crying.*

BENEDICK

Lady Beatrice, have you wept all this while?

*He hands her a handkerchief; she takes it and uses it to wipe
her eyes.*

BEATRICE
> Yea, and I will weep a while longer.

BENEDICK *(comes closer to Beatrice)*
> I do love nothing in the world so well as you:
> *(long pause)* is not that strange?

BEATRICE *(turns toward him, smiling)*
> You have stayed me in a happy hour: I was about to
> protest I loved you.

BENEDICK
> Come, bid me do any thing for thee.

BEATRICE
> Kill Claudio.

BENEDICK *(pauses, laughs a little, then realizes she is serious)*
> Ha! not for the wide world.

BEATRICE
> You kill me to deny it. Farewell.

She starts to leave stage left, but **BENEDICK** *holds her arm gently to stop her.*

BENEDICK
> Is Claudio thine enemy?

BEATRICE *(pulls away from him, animated)*
> Is he not approved in the height a villain, that hath
> slandered, scorned, dishonoured my kinswoman?
> > *(turns toward audience, takes a couple of
> > steps downstage)*
> —O God, that I were a man! I would eat his heart in
> the market-place.

I cannot be a man with wishing, therefore I will die a woman with grieving. *(puts her head in her hands)*

BENEDICK

Tarry, good Beatrice. By this hand, I love thee. *(offers his hand, which she turns away from)*

BEATRICE

Use it for my love some other way than swearing by it.

BENEDICK

Think you in your soul the Count Claudio hath wronged Hero?

BEATRICE *(looking at him straight in the eye)*
Yea, as sure as I have a thought or a soul.

BENEDICK

Enough, I am engaged; I will challenge him. I will kiss your hand, and so I leave you. By this hand, Claudio shall render me a dear account. Go, comfort your cousin: I must say she is dead: and so, *(kisses her hand)*, farewell.

Exit **BENEDICK** *stage right.*

BEATRICE *watches him as he leaves, smiles, and exits stage left.*

✳ **SCENE 5.** (ACT IV, SCENE II)

A prison.

NARRATOR *enters from rear curtain and walks downstage center.*

> Constable Dogberry arrests Conrade and
> manhandles English.

Exit **NARRATOR** *stage right.*

Enter **DOGBERRY** *with* **CONRADE** *from stage rear.* **CONRADE'S**
hands are tied and **DOGBERRY** *has him on a rope.*

DOGBERRY
> Come, let him be opinioned. *(sees that nobody is
> around; shrugs)*

CONRADE
> Off, coxcomb! *(pulls away from him)*

DOGBERRY
> God's my life, where's the sexton? let him write
> down the prince's officer coxcomb. Come, bind
> them. *(there is nobody there)*
> *(to* **CONRADE***)* Thou naughty varlet!

CONRADE *(yelling)*
> Away! you are an ass, you are an ass.

ALL *(from backstage, and startling* **DOGBERRY***)*
> You are an ass.

DOGBERRY

Dost thou not suspect my place? dost thou not
suspect my years? O that the Sexton were here to
write me down an ass!
(to audience) But, masters, remember that I am an
ass; though it be not written down, yet forget not
that I am an ass.
(to CONRADE*)* No, thou villain, thou art full of piety,
as shall be proved upon thee by good witness.
*(takes a step on each of these descriptions, pulling
    poor* CONRADE *with him)*
I am a wise fellow, and, which is more, an officer,
and, which is more, a householder, and, which is
more, as pretty a piece of flesh as any is in Messina,
(turns to CONRADE*)* and one that knows the law, go to;
(pokes CONRADE, *who backs up, annoyed)* and a rich
fellow enough, go to;
(pokes CONRADE, *who backs up once more)* and a fellow
that hath had losses, and one that hath two gowns and
every thing handsome about him. Bring him away.
(looks around and sees that they are alone) O that I
had been writ down an ass!

Exit DOGBERRY *and* CONRADE *stage right, with the latter hurry-
ing behind, trying not to get dragged by the rope.*

✳ SCENE 6. (ACT V, SCENE IV)

A room in Leonato's house.

NARRATOR *enters from rear curtain and walks downstage center.*

> We are at another wedding. Let's hope this one turns
> out better than the last one!

Exit **NARRATOR** *stage right.*

Enter **LEONATO, ANTONIO, BENEDICK, FRIAR FRANCIS, BEATRICE,
MARGARET, URSULA,** *and* **HERO** *from rear.*

FRIAR FRANCIS
> Did I not tell you she was innocent?

LEONATO
> So are the prince and Claudio, who accused her.

ANTONIO
> Well, I am glad that all things sort so well.

LEONATO
> Well, daughter, and you gentle-women all,
> Withdraw into a chamber by yourselves,
> And when I send for you, come hither mask'd.

Exit **LADIES** *stage right.*

FRIAR FRANCIS
> Here comes the prince and Claudio.

Enter DON PEDRO *and* CLAUDIO *from rear. Those already onstage move stage right, and the entering men stand to their left with* CLAUDIO *in the center.*

DON PEDRO

> Good morrow to this fair assembly.

LEONATO

> Good morrow, prince; good morrow, Claudio:
> We here attend you. Are you yet determined
> To-day to marry with my brother's daughter?

CLAUDIO

> I'll hold my mind.

LEONATO

> Call her forth, brother; here's the friar ready.

ANTONIO *beckons offstage for* LADIES *to enter.*

SOUND OPERATOR *plays* Sound Cue #2 *("Wedding March").*

Enter LADIES, *masked, from stage right.*

CLAUDIO

> Which is the lady I must seize upon?

ANTONIO

> This same is she, and I do give you her.

ANTONIO *brings* HERO *forward, center, across from* CLAUDIO.

CLAUDIO

> Give me your hand: before this holy friar,
> I am your husband, if you like of me.

HERO

And when I lived, I was your other wife:
(unmasking) And when you loved, you were my
other husband.

CLAUDIO

Another Hero!

HERO

One Hero died defiled, but I do live,
And surely as I live, I am a maid.

DON PEDRO

The former Hero! Hero that is dead!

LEONATO

She died, my lord, but whiles her slander lived.

FRIAR FRANCIS

All this amazement can I qualify:
When after that the holy rites are ended.

BENEDICK

Soft and fair, friar. Which is Beatrice?

BEATRICE *(unmasking)*

I answer to that name. What is your will?

BENEDICK

Do not you love me?

MARGARET, URSULA, *and* BEATRICE *all laugh.*

BEATRICE

Why, no; no more than reason.

BENEDICK

Why, then your uncle and the prince and Claudio
Have been deceived; they swore you did.

BEATRICE

Do not you love me?

BENEDICK

Troth, no; no more than reason.

BEATRICE

Why, then my cousin Margaret and Ursula
Are much deceived; for they did swear you did.

BENEDICK

They swore that you were almost sick for me.

BEATRICE

They swore that you were well-nigh dead for me.

BENEDICK

'Tis no such matter. Then you do not love me?

BEATRICE

No, truly, but in friendly recompense.

LEONATO

Come, cousin, I am sure you love the gentleman.

CLAUDIO

And I'll be sworn upon't that he loves her;
For here's a paper written in his hand,
A halting sonnet of his own pure brain,
Fashion'd to Beatrice.

BENEDICK *tries to grab the letter, but* CLAUDIO *keeps it away from him.*

HERO

> And here's another
> Writ in my cousin's hand, stolen from her pocket,
> Containing her affection unto Benedick.

BEATRICE *tries to grab the letter, but* HERO *keeps it away from her.*

BENEDICK

> A miracle! here's our own hands against our hearts.
> Come, I will have thee; but, by this light, I take thee
> for pity.

BEATRICE

> I would not deny you; but, by this good day, I yield
> upon great persuasion; and partly to save your life,
> for I was told you were in a consumption.

BENEDICK

> Peace! I will stop your mouth. *(kisses* BEATRICE*)*

DON PEDRO

> How dost thou, Benedick, the married man?

BENEDICK

> In brief, Man is a giddy thing, and this is my
> > conclusion.
> *(to* CLAUDIO*)* Come, come, we are friends: let's have
> a dance ere we are married, that we may lighten our
> own hearts and our wives' heels.

LEONATO

> We'll have dancing afterward.

BENEDICK
> First, of my word; therefore play, music.

Enter BALTHASAR *from rear, breathless and excited.*

BALTHASAR
> My lord, your brother John is ta'en in flight,
> And brought with armed men back to Messina.

All other cast members begin to enter, forming a line.

BENEDICK
> Think not on him till to-morrow:
> I'll devise thee brave punishments for him.
> Strike up, pipers.

ALL *(singing The Song in unison, stepping together in rhythm)*
> Sigh no more, ladies, sigh no more,
> Men were deceivers ever,
> One foot in sea and one on shore,
> To one thing constant never:
> Then sigh not so, but let them go,
> And be you blithe and bonny,
> Converting all your sounds of woe
> Into Hey nonny, nonny.

All hold hands and take a bow. Exeunt.

✳ PERFORMING SHAKESPEARE

HOW *THE 30-MINUTE SHAKESPEARE* WAS BORN

In 1981 I performed a "Shakespeare Juggling" piece called "To Juggle
or Not To Juggle" at the first Folger Library Secondary School Shakespeare Festival. The audience consisted of about 200 Washington,
D.C. area high school students who had just performed thirty-minute
versions of Shakespeare plays for each other and were jubilant over the
experience. I was dressed in a jester's outfit, and my job was to enter-
tain them. I juggled and jested and played with Shakespeare's words,
notably Hamlet's "To be or not to be" soliloquy, to very enthusiastic
response. I was struck by how much my "Shakespeare Juggling" reso-
nated with a group who had just performed Shakespeare themselves.
"Getting" Shakespeare is a heady feeling, especially for adolescents,
and I am continually delighted at how much joy and satisfaction
young people derive from performing Shakespeare. Simply reading
and studying this great playwright does not even come close to
inspiring the kind of enthusiasm that comes from performance.

Surprisingly, many of these students were not "actor types." A
good percentage of the students performing Shakespeare that day
were part of an English class which had rehearsed the plays during
class time. Fifteen years later, when I first started directing plays in
D.C. public schools as a Teaching Artist with the Folger Shakespeare
Library, I entered a ninth grade English class as a guest and spent
two or three days a week for two or three months preparing students for the Folger's annual Secondary School Shakespeare Festival.
I have conducted this annual residency with the Folger ever since.
Every year for seven action-packed days, eight groups of students

between grades seven and twelve tread the boards onstage at the Folger's Elizabethan Theatre, a grand recreation of a sixteenth-century venue with a three-tiered gallery, carved oak columns, and a sky-painted canopy.

As noted on the Folger website (www.folger.edu), "The festival is a celebration of the Bard, not a competition. Festival commentators—drawn from the professional theater and Shakespeare education communities—recognize exceptional performances, student directors, and good spirit amongst the students with selected awards at the end of each day. They are also available to share feedback with the students."

My annual Folger Teaching Artist engagement, directing a Shakespeare play in a public high school English class, is the most challenging and the most rewarding thing I do all year. I hope this book can bring you the same rewards.

GETTING STARTED

GAMES

How can you get an English class (or any other group of young people, or even adults) to start the seemingly daunting task of performing a Shakespeare play? You have already successfully completed the critical first step, which is buying this book. You hold in your hand a performance-ready, thirty-minute cutting of a Shakespeare play, with stage directions to get the actors moving about the stage purposefully. But it's a good idea to warm the group up with some theater games.

One good initial exercise is called "Positive/Negative Salutations." Students stand in two lines facing each other (four or five students in each line) and, reading from index cards, greet each other, first with a "Positive" salutation in Shakespeare's language (using actual phrases from the plays), followed by a "negative" greeting.

Additionally, short vocal exercises are an essential part of the preparation process. The following is a very simple and effective vocal warm-up: Beginning with the number two, have the whole group count to twenty using increments of two (i.e., "Two, four, six . . ."). Increase the volume slightly with each number, reaching top volume with "twenty," and then decrease the volume while counting back down, so that the students are practically whispering when they arrive again at "two." This exercise teaches dynamics and allows them to get loud as a group without any individual pressure. Frequently during a rehearsal period, if a student is mumbling inaudibly, I will refer back to this exercise as a reminder that we can and often do belt it out!

"Stomping Words" is a game that is very helpful at getting a handle on Shakespeare's rhythm. Choose a passage in iambic pentameter and have the group members walk around the room in a circle, stomping their feet on the second beat of each line:

Two **house**-holds, **both** a-**like** in **dig**-nity
In **fair** Ve-**rona Where** we **lay** our **scene**

Do the same thing with a prose passage, and have the students discuss their experience with it, including points at which there is an extra beat, etc., and what, if anything, it might signify.

I end every vocal warm-up with a group reading of one of the speeches from the play, emphasizing diction and projection, bouncing off consonants, and encouraging the group members to listen to each other so that they can speak the lines together in unison. For variety I will throw in some classic "tongue twisters" too, such as, "The sixth sheik's sixth sheep is sick."

The Folger Shakespeare Library's website (http://www.folger.edu) and their book series *Shakespeare Set Free,* edited by Peggy O'Brien, are two great resources for getting started with a performance-based teaching of Shakespeare in the classroom. The Folger website has numerous helpful resources and activities, many submitted by teachers, for helping a class actively participate in the process of getting to know a Shakespeare play. For more simple theater games, Viola Spolin's *Theatre Games for the Classroom* is very helpful, as is one I use frequently, *Theatre Games for Young Performers*.

HATS AND PROPS

Introducing a few hats and props early in the process is a good way to get the action going. Hats, in particular, provide a nice avenue for giving young actors a non-verbal way of getting into character. In the opening weeks, when students are still holding onto their scripts, a hat can give an actor a way to "feel" like a character. Young actors are natural masters at injecting their own personality into what they wear, and even small choices made with how a hat is worn (jauntily, shadily, cockily, mysteriously) provide a starting point for discussion of specific characters, their traits, and their relationships with other characters. All such discussions always lead back to one thing: the text. "Mining the text" is consistently the best strategy for uncovering the mystery of Shakespeare's language. That is where all the answers lie: in the words themselves.

WHAT DO THE WORDS MEAN?

It is essential that young actors know what they are saying when they recite Shakespeare. If not, they might as well be scat singing, riffing on sounds and rhythm but not conveying a specific meaning. The real question is: What do the words mean? The answer is multifaceted, and can be found in more than one place. The New Folger Library paperback editions of the plays themselves (edited by Barbara Mowat and Paul Werstine, Washington Square Press) are a great resource for understanding Shakespeare's words and passages and "translating" them into modern English. These editions also contain chapters on Shakespeare's language, his life, his theater, a "Modern Perspective," and further reading. There is a wealth of scholarship embedded in these wonderful books, and I make it a point to read them cover to cover before embarking on a play-directing project. At the very least, it is a good idea for any adult who intends to direct a Shakespeare play with a group of students to go through the explanatory notes that appear on the pages facing the text. These explanatory notes are an indispensable "translation tool."

The best way to get students to understand what Shakespeare's words mean is to ask them what they think they mean. Students have their own associations with the words and with how they sound and feel. The best ideas on how to perform Shakespeare often come directly from the students, not from anybody else's notion. If a student has an idea or feeling about a word or passage, and it resonates with her emotionally, physically, or spiritually, then Shakespeare's words can be a vehicle for her feelings. That can result in some powerful performances!

I make it my job as director to read the explanatory notes in the Folger text, but I make it clear to the students that almost "anything goes" when trying to understand Shakespeare. There are no wrong interpretations. Students have their own experiences, with some shared and some uniquely their own. If someone has an association with the phrase "canker-blossom," or if the words make that student or his character feel or act a certain way, then that is the "right" way to decipher it.

I encourage the students to refer to the Folger text's explanatory notes and to keep a pocket dictionary handy. Young actors must attach some meaning to every word or line they recite. If I feel an actor is glossing over a word, I will stop him and ask him what he is saying. If he doesn't know, we will figure it out together as a group.

PROCESS VS. PRODUCT

The process of learning Shakespeare by performing one of his plays is more important than whether everybody remembers his lines or whether somebody misses a cue or an entrance. But my Teaching Artist residencies have always had the end goal of a public performance for about 200 other students, so naturally the performance starts to take precedence over the process somewhere around dress rehearsal in the students' minds. It is my job to make sure the actors are prepared—otherwise they will remember the embarrassing moment of a public mistake and not the glorious triumph of owning a Shakespeare play.

In one of my earlier years of play directing, I was sitting in the audience as one of my narrators stood frozen on stage for at least a minute, trying to remember her opening line. I started scrambling in my backpack below my seat for a script, at last prompting her from the audience. Despite her fine performance, that embarrassing moment is all she remembered from the whole experience. Since then I have made sure to assign at least one person to prompt from backstage if necessary. Additionally, I inform the entire cast that if somebody is dying alone out there, it is okay to rescue him or her with an offstage prompt.

There is always a certain amount of stage fright that will accompany a performance, especially a public one for an unfamiliar audience. As a director, I live with stage fright as well, even though I am not appearing on stage. The only antidote to this is work and preparation. If a young actor is struggling with her lines, I make sure to arrange for a session where we run lines over the telephone. I try to set up a buddy system so that students can run lines with their peers, and this often works well. But if somebody does not have a "buddy," I will personally make the time to help out myself. As I assure my students from the outset, I am not going to let them fail or embarrass themselves. They need an experienced leader. And if the leader has experience in teaching but not in directing Shakespeare, then he needs this book!

It is a good idea to culminate in a public performance, as opposed to an in-class project, even if it is only for another classroom. Student actors want to show their newfound Shakespearian thespian skills to an outside group, and this goal motivates them to do a good job. In that respect, "product" is important. Another wonderful bonus to performing a play is that it is a unifying group effort. Students learn teamwork. They learn to give focus to another actor when he is speaking, and to play off of other characters. I like to end each performance with the entire cast reciting a passage in unison. This is a powerful ending, one that reaffirms the unity of the group.

SEEING SHAKESPEARE PERFORMED

It is very helpful for young actors to see Shakespeare performed by a group of professionals, whether they are appearing live on stage (preferable but not always possible) or on film. Because an entire play can take up two or more full class periods, time may be an issue. I am fortunate because thanks to a local foundation that underwrites theater education in the schools, I have been able to take my school groups to a Folger Theatre matinee of the play that they are performing. I always pick a play that is being performed locally that season. But not all group leaders are that lucky. Fortunately, there is the Internet, specifically YouTube. A quick YouTube search for "Shakespeare" can unearth thousands of results, many appropriate for the classroom.

The first "Hamlet" result showed an 18-year-old African-American actor on the streets of Camden, New Jersey, delivering a riveting performance of Hamlet's "The play's the thing." The second clip was from *Cat Head Theatre,* an animation of cats performing Hamlet. Of course, YouTube boasts not just alley cats and feline thespians, but also clips by true legends of the stage, such as John Gielgud and Richard Burton. These clips can be saved and shown in classrooms, providing useful inspiration.

One advantage of the amazing variety of clips available on YouTube is that students can witness the wide range of interpretations for any given scene, speech, or character in Shakespeare, thus freeing them from any preconceived notion that there is a "right" way to do it. Furthermore, modern interpretations of the Bard may appeal to those who are put off by the "thees and thous" of Elizabethan speech.

By seeing Shakespeare performed either live or on film, students are able to hear the cadence, rhythm, vocal dynamics, and pronunciation of the language, and they can appreciate the life that other actors breathe into the characters. They get to see the story told dramatically, which inspires them to tell their own version.

PUTTING IT ALL TOGETHER

THE STEPS

After a few sessions of theater games to warm up the group, it's time to begin the process of casting the play. Each play cutting in *The 30-Minute Shakespeare* series includes a cast list and a sample program, demonstrating which parts have been divided. Cast size is generally between twelve and thirty students, with major roles frequently assigned to more than one performer. In other words, one student may play Juliet in the first scene, another in the second scene, and yet another in the third. This will distribute the parts evenly so that there is no "star of the show." Furthermore, this prevents actors from being burdened with too many lines. If I have an actor who is particularly talented or enthusiastic, I will give her a bigger role. It is important to go with the grain—one cast member's enthusiasm can be contagious.

I provide the performer of each shared role with a similar headpiece and/or cape, so that the audience can keep track of the characters. When there are sets of twins, I try to use blue shirts and red shirts, so that the audience has at least a fighting chance of figuring it out! Other than these costume consistencies, I rely on the text and the audience's observance to sort out the doubling of characters. Generally, the audience can follow because we are telling the story.

Some participants are shy and do not wish to speak at all on stage. To these students I assign non-speaking parts and technical roles such as sound operator and stage manager. However, I always get everybody on stage at some point, even if it is just for the final group speech, because I want every group member to experience what it is like to be on a stage as part of an ensemble.

CASTING THE PLAY

Young people can be self-conscious and nervous with "formal" auditions, especially if they have little or no acting experience.

I conduct what I call an "informal" audition process. I hand out a questionnaire asking students if there is any particular role that they desire, whether they play a musical instrument. To get a feel for them as people, I also ask them to list one or two hobbies or interests. Occasionally this will inform my casting decisions. If someone can juggle, and the play has the part of a Fool, that skill may come in handy. Dancing or martial arts abilities can also be applied to roles.

For the auditions, I do not use the cut script. I have students stand and read from the Folger edition of the complete text in order to hear how they fare with the longer passages. I encourage them to breathe and carry their vocal energy all the way to the end of a long line of text. I also urge them to play with diction, projection, modulation, and dynamics, elements of speech that we have worked on in our vocal warm-ups and theater games.

I base my casting choices largely on reading ability, vocal strength, and enthusiasm for the project. If someone has requested a particular role, I try to honor that request. I explain that even with a small part, an actor can create a vivid character that adds a lot to the play. Wide variations in personality types can be utilized: if there are two students cast as Romeo, one brooding and one effusive, I try to put the more brooding Romeo in an early lovelorn scene, and place the effusive Romeo in the balcony scene. Occasionally one gets lucky, and the doubling of characters provides a way to match personality types with different aspects of a character's personality. But also be aware of the potential serendipity of non-traditional casting. For example, I have had one of the smallest students in the class play a powerful Othello. True power comes from within!

Generally, I have more females than males in a class, so women are more likely (and more willing) to play male characters than vice versa.

Rare is the high school boy who is brave enough to play a female character, which is unfortunate because it can reap hilarious results.

GET OUTSIDE HELP

Every time there is a fight scene in one of the plays I am directing, I call on my friend Michael Tolaydo, a professional actor and theater professor at St. Mary's College, who is an expert in all aspects of theater, including fight choreography. Not only does Michael stage the fight, but he does so in a way that furthers the action of the play, highlighting character's traits and bringing out the best in the student actors. Fight choreography must be done by an expert or somebody could get hurt. In the absence of such help, super slow-motion fights are always a safe bet and can be quite effective, especially when accompanied by a soundtrack on the boom box.

During dress rehearsals I invite my friend Hilary Kacser. a Washington-area actor and dialect coach for two decades. Because I bring her in late in the rehearsal process, I have her direct her comments to me, which I then filter and relay to the cast. This avoids confusing the cast with a second set of directions. This caveat only applies to general directorial comments from outside visitors. Comments on specific artistic disciplines such as dance, music, and stage combat can come from the outside experts themselves.

If you work in a school, you might have helpful resources within your own building, such as a music or dance teacher who could contribute their expertise to a scene. If nobody is available in your school, try seeking out a member of the local professional theater. Many local performing artists will be glad to help, and the students are usually thrilled to have a visit from a professional performer.

LET STUDENTS BRING THEMSELVES INTO THE PLAY

The best ideas often come from the students themselves. If a young actor has a notion of how to play a scene, I will always give that idea a try. In a rehearsal of *Henry IV, Part 1,* one traveler jumped into the other's arms when they were robbed. It got a huge laugh. This was something that they did on instinct. We kept that bit for the performance, and it worked wonderfully.

As a director, you have to foster an environment in which that kind of spontaneity can occur. The students have to feel safe to experiment. In the same production of *Henry IV*, Falstaff and Hal invented a little fist bump "secret handshake" to use in the battle scene. The students were having fun and bringing parts of themselves into the play. Shakespeare himself would have approved. When possible I try to err on the side of fun because if the young actors are having fun, then they will commit themselves to the project. The beauty of the language, the story, the characters, and the pathos will follow.

There is a balance to be achieved here, however. In that same production of *Henry IV, Part 1*, the student who played Bardolph was having a great time with her character. She carried a leather wineskin around and offered it up to the other characters in the tavern. It was a prop with which she developed a comic relationship. At the end of our thirty-minute *Henry IV, Part 1*, I added a scene from *Henry IV, Part 2* as a coda: The new King Henry V (formerly Falstaff's drinking and carousing buddy Hal) rejects Falstaff, banishing him from within ten miles of the King. It is a sad and sobering moment, one of the most powerful in the play.

But at the performance, in the middle of the King's rejection speech (played by a female student, and her only speech), Bardolph offered her flask to King Henry and got a big laugh, thus not only upstaging the King but also undermining the seriousness and poignancy of the whole scene. She did not know any better; she was bringing herself to the character as I had been encouraging her to do. But it was inappropriate, and in subsequent seasons, if I foresaw something like that happening as an individual joyfully occupied a character, I attempted to prevent it. Some things we cannot predict. Now I make sure to issue a statement warning against changing any of the blocking on show day, and to watch out for upstaging one's peers.

FOUR FORMS OF ENGAGEMENT: VOCAL, EMOTIONAL, PHYSICAL, AND INTELLECTUAL

When directing a Shakespeare play with a group of students, I always start with the words themselves because the words have the power to engage the emotions, mind, and body. Also, I start with the words in action, as in the previously mentioned exercise, "Positive and Negative Salutations." Students become physically engaged; their bodies react to the images the words evoke. The words have the power to trigger a switch in both the teller and the listener, eliciting both an emotional and physical reaction. I have never heard a student utter the line "Fie! Fie! You counterfeit, you puppet you!" without seeing him change before my eyes. His spine stiffens, his eyes widen, and his fingers point menacingly.

Having used Shakespeare's words to engage the students emotionally and physically, one can then return to the text for a more reflective discussion of what the words mean to us personally. I always make sure to leave at least a few class periods open for discussion of the text, line by line, to ensure that students understand intellectually what they feel viscerally. The advantage to a performance-based teaching of Shakespeare is that by engaging students vocally, emotionally, and physically, it is then much easier to engage them intellectually because they are invested in the words, the characters, and the story. We always start on our feet, and later we sit and talk.

SIX ELEMENTS OF DRAMA: PLOT, CHARACTER, THEME, DICTION, MUSIC, AND SPECTACLE

Over two thousand years ago, Aristotle's *Poetics* outlined six elements of drama, in order of importance: Plot, Character, Theme, Diction, Music, and Spectacle. Because Shakespeare was foremost a playwright, it is helpful to take a brief look at these six elements as they relate to directing a Shakespeare play in the classroom.

PLOT (ACTION)

To Aristotle, plot was the most important element. One of the purposes of *The 30-Minute Shakespeare* is to provide a script that tells Shakespeare's stories, as opposed to concentrating on one scene. In a thirty-minute edit of a Shakespeare play, some plot elements are necessarily omitted. For the sake of a full understanding of the characters' relationships and motivations, it is helpful to make short plot summaries of each scene so that students are aware of their characters' arcs throughout the play. The scene descriptions in the Folger editions are sufficient to fill in the plot holes. Students can read the descriptions aloud during class time to ensure that the story is clear and that no plot elements are neglected. Additionally, there are one-page charts in the Folger editions of *Shakespeare Set Free,* indicating characters' relations graphically, with lines connecting families and factions to give students a visual representation of what can often be complex interrelationships, particularly in Shakespeare's history plays.

Young actors love action. That is why *The 30-Minute Shakespeare* includes dynamic blocking (stage direction) that allows students to tell the story in a physically dramatic fashion. Characters' movements on the stage are always motivated by the text itself.

CHARACTER

I consider myself a facilitator and a director more than an acting teacher. I want the students' understanding of their characters to spring from the text and the story. From there, I encourage them to consider how their character might talk, walk, stand, sit, eat, and drink. I also urge students to consider characters' motivations, objectives, and relationships, and I will ask pointed questions to that end during the rehearsal process. I try not to show the students how I would perform a scene, but if no ideas are forthcoming from anybody in the class, I will suggest a minimum of two possibilities for how the character might respond.

At times students may want more guidance and examples. Over thirteen years of directing plays in the classroom, I have wavered between wanting all the ideas to come from the students, and deciding that I need to be more of a "director," telling them what I would like to see them doing. It is a fine line, but in recent years I have decided that if I don't see enough dynamic action or characterization, I will step in and "direct" more. But I always make sure to leave room for students to bring themselves into the characters because their own ideas are invariably the best.

THEME (THOUGHTS, IDEAS)

In a typical English classroom, theme will be a big topic for discussion of a Shakespeare play. Using a performance-based method of teaching Shakespeare, an understanding of the play's themes develops from "mining the text" and exploring Shakespeare's words and his story. If the students understand what they are saying and how that relates to their characters and the overall story, the plays' themes will emerge clearly. We always return to the text itself. There are a number of elegant computer programs, such as www.wordle.net, that will count the number of recurring words in a passage and illustrate them graphically. For example, if the word "jealousy" comes up more than any other word in *Othello*, it will appear in a larger font. Seeing the words displayed by size in this way can offer up illuminating insights into the interaction between words in the text and the play's themes. Your computer-minded students might enjoy searching for such tidbits. There are more internet tools and websites in the Additional Resources section at the back of this book.

I cannot overstress the importance of acting out the play in understanding its themes. By embodying the roles of Othello and Iago and reciting their words, students do not simply comprehend the themes intellectually, but understand them kinesthetically, physically, and emotionally. They are essentially *living* the characters' jealousy, pride, and feelings about race. The themes of appearance vs.

reality, good vs. evil, honesty, misrepresentation, and self-knowledge (or lack thereof) become physically felt as well as intellectually understood. Performing Shakespeare delivers a richer understanding than that which comes from just reading the play. Students can now relate the characters' conflicts to their own struggles.

DICTION (LANGUAGE)

If I had to cite one thing I would like my actors to take from their experience of performing a play by William Shakespeare, it is an appreciation and understanding of the beauty of Shakespeare's language. The language is where it all begins and ends. Shakespeare's stories are dramatic, his characters are rich and complex, and his settings are exotic and fascinating, but it is through his language that these all achieve their richness. This leads me to spend more time on language than on any other element of the performance.

Starting with daily vocal warm-ups, many of them using parts of the script or other Shakespearean passages, I consistently emphasize the importance of the words. Young actors often lack experience in speaking clearly and projecting their voices outward, so in addition to comprehension, I emphasize projection, diction, breathing, pacing, dynamics, coloring of words, and vocal energy. *Theatre Games for Young Performers* contains many effective vocal exercises, as does the Folger's *Shakespeare Set Free* series. Consistent emphasis on all aspects of Shakespeare's language, especially on how to speak it effectively, is the most important element to any Shakespeare performance with a young cast.

MUSIC

A little music can go a long way in setting a mood for a thirty-minute Shakespeare play. I usually open the show with a short passage of music to set the tone. Thirty seconds of music played on a boom box operated by a student can provide a nice introduction to the play, create an atmosphere for the audience, and give the actors a sense of place and feeling.

iTunes is a good starting point for choosing your music. Typing in "Shakespeare" or "Hamlet" or "jealousy" (if you are going for a theme) will result in an excellent selection of aural performance enhancers at the very reasonable price of ninety-nine cents each (or free of charge, see Additional Resources section). Likewise, fight sounds, foreboding sounds, weather sounds (rain, thunder), trumpet sounds, etc. are all readily available online at affordable cost. I typically include three sound cues in a play, just enough to enhance but not overpower a production. The boom box operator sits on the far right or left of the stage, not backstage, so he can see the action. This also has the added benefit of having somebody out there with a script, capable of prompting in a pinch.

SPECTACLE

Aristotle considered spectacle the least important aspect of drama. Students tend to be surprised at this since we are used to being bombarded with production values on TV and video, often at the expense of substance. In my early days of putting on student productions, I would find myself hamstrung by my own ambitions in the realm of scenic design.

A simple bench or two chairs set on the stage are sufficient. The sense of "place" can be achieved through language and acting. Simple set dressing, a few key props, and some tasteful, emblematic costume pieces will go a long way toward providing all the "spectacle" you need.

In the stage directions to the plays in *The 30-Minute Shakespeare* series, I make frequent use of two large pillars stage left and right at the Folger Shakespeare Library's Elizabethan Theatre. I also have characters frequently entering and exiting from "stage rear." Your stage will have a different layout. Take a good look at the performing space you will be using and see if there are any elements that can be incorporated into your own stage directions. Is there a balcony? Can characters enter from the audience? (Make sure that they can get there from backstage, unless you want them waiting in the lobby until their entrance, which may be impractical.) If possible, make sure to rehearse in that space a few times to fix any technical issues and perhaps discover a few fun staging variations that will add pizzazz and dynamics to your own show.

The real spectacle is in the telling of the tale. Wooden swords are handy for characters that need them. Students should be warned at the outset that playing with swords outside of the scene is verboten. Letters, moneybags, and handkerchiefs should all have plentiful duplicates kept in a small prop box, as well as with a stage manager, because they tend to disappear in the hands of adolescents. After every rehearsal and performance, I recommend you personally sweep the rehearsal or performance area immediately for stray props. It is amazing what gets left behind.

Ultimately, the performances are about language and human drama, not set pieces, props, and special effects. Fake blood, glitter, glass, and liquids have no place on the stage; they are a recipe for disaster, or, at the very least, a big mess. On the other hand, the props that are employed can often be used effectively to convey character, as in Bardolph's aforementioned relationship with his wineskin.

PITFALLS AND SOLUTIONS

Putting on a play in a high school classroom is not easy. There are problems with enthusiasm, attitude, attention, and line memorization, to name a few. As anybody who has directed a play will tell you, it is always darkest before the dawn. My experience is that after one or two days of utter despair just before the play goes up, show day breaks and the play miraculously shines. To quote a recurring gag in one of my favorite movies, *Shakespeare in Love:* "It's a mystery."

ENTHUSIASM, FRUSTRATION, AND DISCIPLINE

Bring the enthusiasm yourself. Feed on the energy of the eager students, and others will pick up on that. Keep focused on the task at hand. Arrive prepared. Enthusiasm comes as you make headway. Ultimately, it helps to remind the students that a play is fun. I try to focus on the positive attributes of the students, rather than the ones that drive me crazy. This is easier said than done, but it is important. One season, I yelled at the group two days in a row. On day two of yelling, they tuned me out, and it took me a while to win them back. I learned my lesson; since then I've tried not to raise my voice out of anger or frustration. As I grow older and more mature, it is important for me to lead by example. It has been years since I yelled at a student group. If I am disappointed in their work or their behavior, I will express my disenchantment in words, speaking from the heart as somebody who cares about them and cares about our performance and our experience together. I find that fundamentally, young people want to please, to do well, and to be liked. If there is a serious discipline problem, I will hand it over to the regular classroom teacher, the administrator, or the parent.

LINE MEMORIZATION

Students may have a hard time memorizing lines. In these cases, see if you can pair them up with a "buddy" and existing friend who will run lines with them in person or over the phone after school. If students do not have such a "buddy," I volunteer to run lines with them myself. If serious line memorization problems arise that cannot be solved through work, then two students can switch parts if it is early enough in the rehearsal process. For doubled roles, the scene with fewer lines can go to the actor who is having memorization problems. Additionally, a few passages or lines can be cut. Again, it is important to address these issues early. Later cuts become more problematic as other actors have already memorized their cues. I have had to do late cuts about twice in thirteen years. While they have gotten us out of jams, it is best to assess early whether a student will have line memorization problems, and deal with the problem sooner rather than later.

In production, always keep several copies of the script backstage, as well as cheat sheets indicating cues, entrances, and scene changes. Make a prop list, indicating props for each scene, as well as props that are the responsibility of individual actors. Direct the Stage Manager and an Assistant Stage Manager to keep track of these items, and on show days, personally double-check if you can.

In thirteen years of preparing an inner-city public high school English class for a public performance on a field trip to the Folger Secondary School Shakespeare Festival, my groups and I have been beset by illness, emotional turmoil, discipline problems, stage fright, adolescent angst, midlife crises (not theirs), and all manner of other emergencies, including acts of God and nature. Despite the difficulties and challenges inherent in putting on a Shakespeare play with a group of young people, one amazing fact stands out in my experience. Here is how many times a student has been absent for show day: Zero. Somehow, everybody has always made it to the show, and the show has gone on. How can this be? It's a mystery.

✳ PERFORMANCE NOTES: *MUCH ADO ABOUT NOTHING*

I directed this performance of *Much Ado About Nothing* in 2006. These notes are the result of my own review of the performance video. They are not intended to be the "definitive" performance notes for all productions of *Much Ado About Nothing*. Your production will be unique to you and your cast. That is the magic of live theater. What is interesting about these notes is that many of the performance details I mention were not part of the original stage directions. They either emerged spontaneously on performance day or were developed by students in rehearsal after the stage directions had been written into the script. Some of these pieces of stage business work like a charm. Others fall flat. Still others are unintentionally hilarious. My favorites are the ones that arise directly from the students themselves, and demonstrate a union between actor and character, as if that individual becomes a vehicle for the character she is playing. To witness a fifteen-year-old young woman "become" Beatrice as Shakespeare's words leave her mouth is a memorable moment indeed.

This version of *Much Ado About Nothing* consisted of a group of twenty-five ninth graders—and only one male! In the middle of the rehearsal period, when I asked the student (who played Benedick) how he was holding up, he grinned widely and responded, "I'm lovin' it!" If only all ninth graders could have that kind of positive attitude. This comedy is characterized by the fun battle of words between Beatrice and Benedick and by the hysterical pranks played on the lovers by their peers. But what gives the script its punch is its flip side: the brutal rejection of Hero by her groom at the altar, and the subsequent ruse (faking her own death) and redemption (Claudio marrying the "substitute" Hero) that follow.

What gives the best comedies their power is often the pain that lurks behind the surface and under the laughter. Such is also the case with the battles between Beatrice and Benedick. Their war of words is amusing, but both have been hurt in love, and the clever verbal barbs they direct at each other are their armor. It is clear from their words that they have a history, and it is not a pretty one. I encourage the actors to play the "word fight" scenes for laughs, but to be aware of the history of hurt that underlies their words and undercuts the humor, ironically making it funnier. How do they achieve this subtlety? Often simply being aware of this nuance, which is readily uncovered by mining the text, is sufficient to allow the actors to give their characters some weight. And it is this weight that makes the lightness lighter! I dwell on this point because it is an important one that can be successfully applied to all comedies.

SCENE 1 (ACT I, SCENE I)

We begin the play with a group scene. As Don Pedro and the soldiers return from the wars, those who have stayed behind cheer and applaud them heartily as they enter. This gives the audience a feel for the relief and joy that accompanies the return from battle. This is also an opportunity for the actor playing Don John to non-verbally indicate his villainy by lurking broodingly in the background of the crowd scenes, conveying his general pleasure with the status quo, and showing his potential for disruption of all things merry.

The stage directions have actors entering from the rear of the stage. These scenes were designed for the Folger Shakespeare Library's Elizabethan stage, which often has a rear entrance for actors. This direction has the advantage of varying the entrances, but it can result in actors "clumping" upstage and not descending far enough downstage to be properly visible and audible to the audience. Over the years, I have tended to scale back "rear entrances," and since there is no guarantee that your performance space will have an available entrance at the rear of the stage, please feel free to use side entrances exclusively.

Having said that, if there is an opportunity at some point for an actor to enter from the rear of the *audience*, this can be an effective and fun way to shake things up while breaking the "third wall." Audiences love being physically close to actors, and if there is an opportunity for a player entering from the audience to somehow interact with someone in the seats (a directed comment, eye contact, etc.) this audience entrance gives us that opportunity. In *Much Ado About Nothing*, Don John is a villain, and therefore it would be not out of character for him to purposefully glare or even menace an audience member for his own delight, which has the added advantage of accentuating his evil nature.

Beatrice and Benedick's interplay in this first scene can be choreographed as a combination of a dance and a duel. Benedick moves toward Beatrice, and sits. She stands. Benedick takes a step toward Beatrice. She responds with a step toward Benedick. Benedick turns his back toward Beatrice, and she turns her back on him. The attraction/repulsion in the text is thus illustrated comically through the blocking, which sets the tone for their entire relationship.

SCENE 2 (ACT II, SCENE III)

This scene should be fun and funny. The humor works best if the hiding Benedick does so in plain view of the conspirators, who should make it clear to the audience that they do indeed see him, but choose not to acknowledge it for the sake of their ruse. When Benedick hides behind the potted plant and tiptoes gradually toward the group, his legs should stick out at the bottom, his head should poke out from the top, and his tiptoeing should be large and exaggerated. When Benedick crawls out from behind the plant, ending up on all fours behind the trio, they may then sit on him as if he is a bench. This is of course, absurd, since any sentient being would be able to discern that he is sitting on a human being, but therein lies the comedy. To heighten the absurdity, Benedick himself may non-verbally express shock and amazement that he is not caught. The blocking indicates that all three actors sit on Benedick simultaneously, but the comedy works well (and might be easier on the poor actor playing Benedick) if only one person sits on him, while the others pretend that they are about to sit, which terrifies Benedick, and then change their minds, which relieves him! It is also very comical if, while he is being sat upon, Benedick makes little grunting sounds.

When Claudio imitates Beatrice with the line, "O, sweet Benedick, God give me patience," he will get a laugh if he uses a goofy, high-pitched parody vocal rather than his own voice.

As the three plotters walk off the stage, Benedick remains on all fours with his buttocks up in the air, and his head and back down on the stage as if he has been crushed. This scene provides a great opportunity to achieve big laughs with few props or costume gimmicks, just dialogue and bodies.

The humor works on two levels, verbal and physical, and it is best to separate the two. The collaborator sits on Benedick. Actors *allow the audience's laughter to subside,* and then speak their lines. Young actors frequently step on their own laughter by reciting the next lines too soon, which not only diminishes the reaction but also prohibits the audience from hearing the dialogue.

For Benedick's final line of the scene ("The world must be peopled"), I asked him to accompany the phrase with a gesture of his choice. Ultimately he chose to stick his fist up in the air with arm outstretched, an action that my generation associates with the "Black Power" salute. The ninth grade actor who played Benedick was African American, and I did not ask him why he chose that move, but it got a laugh. What is interesting is how one motion can impart an interesting and perhaps unexpected interpretation.

Student actors often underperform the final sentence of a monologue. They rush the words and end the speech on a softer note than is necessary or beneficial to the scene. Especially when a soliloquy ends a scene, it is important not to hurry, and to carry the energy to the end of the line. This adds a nice exclamation point to a scene and continues the play's momentum.

SCENE 3 (ACT III, SCENE I)

During a 2006 performance of this version of *Much Ado About Nothing*, a "situation" occurred at the beginning of the third scene. The stage was bare, and no actors were forthcoming. The actress playing the sound cues on the boom box was sitting on the side of stage right, unaware that it was her cue to rise and deliver the Narrator's lines center stage to begin the scene. Nobody backstage was prompting her, and the stage was likely going to remain vacant for some time, so I prompted the actor from my seat in the audience. The scenario was not ideal, but it was far preferable to the void that was facing us at that moment. Directors of youth productions should be ready to step in and come to the rescue if necessary. Nonetheless, over the years I have increased my emphasis on students' preparing to help from backstage, assigning not only the role of stage manager, but also various assistants, whose job it is to keep track of cues, props, entrances, and exits, and to intervene when needed. I post "cue cheat sheets" with the cues that precede actors' entrances, and I leave plenty of scripts backstage.

At the beginning of this scene, the actor playing Hero strode on crisply and clapped her hands three times while calling for Margaret. This actor-driven characterization went a long way toward indicating status and position.

The comedy in this segment is similar to that of the previous scene. Beatrice slowly rises from behind the potted plant, holding two branches to her side. When Margaret sees here, she puts her arms out, imitating a plant, and freezes, which gets a big laugh. Particularly gratifying to the audience in this type of comedy sketch is that they know the three collaborators on stage are in on the gag of tricking Beatrice, but Beatrice herself does not know she is being fooled. The audience loves being in on the joke.

Particularly pivotal is Beatrice's "What fire is in my ears?" speech. It is a touching turning point in the play, as Beatrice's emotions switch from contempt to love for Benedick: "And Benedick, love on; I will requite thee." The actor playing Beatrice must take her time with this speech and avoid dropping the last line of her monologue. The audience will then perceive it for what it is: a declaration of love from a character who has been hitherto loveless.

SCENE 4 (ACT IV, SCENE I)

The wedding scene begins with a slow, marching entrance of the wedding party, accompanied by music. Make sure the actors travel downstage enough to be seen and heard by the audience. Especially in group scenes, there can be "upstage creep," as mentioned earlier, or even "side stage creep." Subsequent stage picture dynamics can emanate from this principle, meaning that once the group is center stage, individual members have room to split off from the group as the text calls for it.

Claudio's rejection of his bride-to-be Hero at the altar is terribly painful, and the blocking in this scene should be powerful enough to support that emotion. Claudio's taking Hero by the shoulders and pushing her back to Leonato is a dramatic physical moment that illustrates the cruelty in the text. As in stage combat, the person being shoved (Hero) should be the person in control. The interchange should be practiced first in super-slow motion. Only after careful rehearsal should the speed be increased, and even then, actors should err on the side of caution. The physical and vocal reaction of the other actors on stage can enhance the perception that Hero was thrown harder than she actually was.

When Claudio says, "She knows the heat of a luxurious bed," other actors in the stage should react audibly with gasps. Benedick can turn his face toward the audience as an aside on, "This looks not like a nuptial." This line should bring a nice laugh and provide some welcome comic relief to an otherwise tense and emotional scene. Many of the most satisfying laughs arrive at otherwise dramatic and poignant moments. The audience has no problem switching gears emotionally, and they may immediately re-enter back into the drama, grateful for a laugh to relieve the tension.

At the end of the scene, when Beatrice instructs Benedick to "kill Claudio," Benedick can laugh as if she is joking, then swiftly turn serious when he realizes that she it is not. This creates a more dynamic theatrical moment than having Benedick take Beatrice seriously initially. I decided to have Benedick kiss Beatrice's hand at the end of the scene. To me, the action illustrates a gallantry heretofore unexplored in Benedick, and supports the text, which paints him as a character with more than one dimension, complex and nuanced, thanks to the genius of Shakespeare.

SCENE 5 (ACT IV, SCENE II)

Dogberry is a unique Shakespearean clown. His misuse of language, combined with his exaggerated self-importance combine to create a hysterical and memorable character. When Conrade says to Dogberry, "You are an ass!" I had the entire cast backstage yell the phrase back to him from offstage, which scares him. Other characters' reactions to Dogberry serve to reinforce his status as a buffoon. When Dogberry pokes Conrade, Conrade pokes back, demonstrating that he does not respect Dogberry's authority. But what is so wonderful about Dogberry as created by Shakespeare is that there is more to him than simply a bumbling fool.

During his classic "write me down an ass" speech where Dogberry enumerates all of his qualities, he arrives at "and one that hath had losses." This provides the actor with an opportunity for a sad, reflective, or bitter moment, thus making bumbling his character richer. He has a backstory, and it might not be an altogether happy one. These moments of "mini gravitas" enhance comedy, for what is laughter without the possibility of tears?

SCENE 6 (ACT V, SCENE IV)

To introduce the final scene in this delightful comedy, the narrator's line, "We are at another wedding; Let's hope this one turns out better than the last one," should be spoken in a matter-of-fact tone for maximum comedic effect. The narrators can serve as "straight men" to the comic actors, delivering lines that can get laughs without unnecessary histrionics.

Upon seeing Hero's unveiled face, Claudio should face the audience as an aside for his line "Another Hero!" In general, asides to the audience should be pointed; actors should turn directly to the audience, including them in the comedy. Actors can be encouraged to experiment with pairing their words with a gesture on key lines. Benedick gets a laugh on "'Tis no such matter" just by tossing his head back a little.

Although my 2006 production included only one male actor, the plot and relationships were believable because the actors committed themselves. A couple of fake beards for Don John and Leonato, applied with spirit gum, can help perpetuate the illusion of maleness. Most of this illusion can be achieved through actors' dedication to their roles and their relationships.

When Beatrice and Benedick finally embraced each other at the end of the play, the entire audience of adolescents and adults responded with a spontaneous "Awww." We were ready for the couple to get together. We cared. We believed in the story and had been swept away by its poetic protagonists. That is the magic of Shakespeare. May it be your magic, too.

✳ *MUCH ADO ABOUT NOTHING:* SET AND PROP LIST

SET PIECES

One bench
Potted plant, large enough to hide behind

PROPS

SCENE 4:
Handkerchief

SCENE 5:
Rope

SCENE 6:
Masks for Ladies (or veils to cover faces)
Two letters

Much Ado About Nothing

By William Shakespeare

Wednesday, March 15th, 2006
Performed by the 4th period 9th Grade English Class
Instructor: Whitney Warren | Guest Director: Mr. Nick Newlin

CAST OF CHARACTERS:

In order of appearance

Narrator (Scenes 1, 4, and 6): Makia Weaver
Beatrice: Jasmin Cook
Balthasar: Arionne' Johnson
Leonato: Keyanna Hymes
Don Pedro: Aisha Friday
Benedick: David Mayers
Don John: Shannon Simms
Claudio: Kelly Dove
Hero: Joi Robins-Monroe
Narrator (Scenes 2, 3, and 5): Arionne' Johnson
Ursula: Iesha Gill
Margaret: Faatima Muhammad
Friar Francis: Jasmine Dyson
Dogberry: Marlene Anderson
Conrade: Makia Weaver
Antonio: Clarke Randolph

Stage Manager: Clarke Randolph

*I had rather hear my dog bark at a crow
than a man swear he loves me.*
—Beatrice

*Til all graces be in one woman,
one woman shall not come in my grace.*
—Benedick

ADDITIONAL RESOURCES

SHAKESPEARE

Shakespeare Set Free: Teaching Romeo and Juliet, Macbeth and a Midsummer Night's Dream
Peggy O'Brien, Ed., Teaching Shakespeare Institute
Washington Square Press
New York, 1993

Shakespeare Set Free: Teaching Hamlet and Henry IV, Part 1
Peggy O'Brien, Ed., Teaching Shakespeare Institute
Washington Square Press
New York, 1994

Shakespeare Set Free: Teaching Twelfth Night and Othello
Peggy O'Brien, Ed., Teaching Shakespeare Institute
Washington Square Press
New York, 1995

The *Shakespeare Set Free* series is an invaluable resource with lesson plans, activites, handouts, and excellent suggestions for rehearsing and performing Shakespeare plays in a classroom setting.

ShakesFear and How to Cure It!
Ralph Alan Cohen
Prestwick House, Inc.
Delaware, 2006

The Friendly Shakespeare: A Thoroughly Painless Guide to the Best of the Bard
Norrie Epstein
Penguin Books
New York, 1994

Brush Up Your Shakespeare!
Michael Macrone
Cader Books
New York, 1990

Shakespeare's Insults: Educating Your Wit
Wayne F. Hill and Cynthia J. Ottchen
Three Rivers Press
New York, 1991

Practical Approaches to Teaching Shakespeare
Peter Reynolds
Oxford University Press
New York, 1991

Scenes From Shakespeare:
A Workbook for Actors
Robin J. Holt
McFarland and Co.
London, 1988

101 Theatre Games for Drama
Teachers, Classroom Teachers
& Directors
Mila Johansen
Players Press Inc.
California, 1994

THEATER AND PERFORMANCE

Impro: Improvisation and the Theatre
Keith Johnstone
Routledge Books
London, 1982

A Dictionary of Theatre Anthropology:
The Secret Art of the Performer
Eugenio Barba and Nicola Savarese
Routledge
London, 1991

THEATER GAMES

Theatre Games for Young Performers
Maria C. Novelly
Meriwether Publishing
Colorado, 1990

Improvisation for the Theater
Viola Spolin
Northwestern University Press
Illinois, 1983

Theater Games for Rehearsal:
A Director's Handbook
Viola Spolin
Northwestern University Press
Illinois, 1985

PLAY DIRECTING

Theater and the Adolescent Actor:
Building a Successful School Program
Camille L. Poisson
Archon Books
Connecticut, 1994

Directing for the Theatre
W. David Sievers
Wm. C. Brown, Co.
Iowa, 1965

The Director's Vision: Play Direction
from Analysis to Production
Louis E. Catron
Mayfield Publishing Co.
California, 1989

INTERNET RESOURCES

http://www.folger.edu
The Folger Shakespeare Library's
website has lesson plans, primary
sources, study guides, images,
workshops, programs for teachers
and students, and much more. The
definitive Shakespeare website for
educators, historians and all lovers
of the Bard.

http://www.shakespeare.mit.edu.
The Complete Works of
William Shakespeare.
All complete scripts for *The
30-Minute Shakespeare* series were
originally downloaded from this site
before editing. Links to other internet
resources.

http://www.LoMonico.com/
Shakespeare-and-Media.htm
http://shakespeare-and-media
.wikispaces.com
Michael LoMonico is Senior
Consultant on National Education
for the Folger Shakespeare Library.
His *Seminar Shakespeare 2.0* offers a
wealth of information on how to use
exciting new approaches and online
resources for teaching Shakespeare.

http://www.freesound.org.
A collaborative database of sounds
and sound effects.

http://www.wordle.net.
A program for creating "word clouds"
from the text that you provide. The
clouds give greater prominence to
words that appear more frequently in
the source text.

http://www.opensourceshakespeare
.org.
This site has good searching capacity.

http://shakespeare.palomar.edu/
default.htm
Excellent links and searches

http://shakespeare.com/
Write like Shakespeare,
Poetry Machine, tag cloud

http://www.shakespeare-online.com/

http://www.bardweb.net/

http://www.rhymezone.com/
shakespeare/
Good searchable word and phrase
finder.
Or by lines:
http://www.rhymezone.com/
shakespeare/toplines/

http://shakespeare.mcgill.ca/
Shakespeare and Performance
research team

http://www.enotes.com/william-
shakespeare

Needless to say, the internet goes on and on with valuable Shakespeare resources.
The ones listed here are excellent starting points and will set you on your way in the
great adventure that is Shakespeare.

NICK NEWLIN has performed a comedy and variety act for international audiences for twenty-seven years. Since 1996, he has conducted an annual play directing residency affiliated with the Folger Shakespeare Library in Washington, D.C. Newlin received a BA with Honors from Harvard University in 1982 and an MA in Theater with an emphasis in Play Directing from the University of Maryland in 1996.

THE 30-MINUTE SHAKESPEARE

A MIDSUMMER NIGHT'S DREAM
978-1-935550-00-6

ROMEO AND JULIET
978-1-935550-01-3

MUCH ADO ABOUT NOTHING
978-1-935550-03-7

MACBETH
978-1-935550-02-0

THE MERRY WIVES OF WINDSOR
978-1-935550-05-1

TWELFTH NIGHT
978-1-935550-04-4

AVAILABLE IN FALL 2010

AS YOU LIKE IT
978-1-935550-06-8

LOVE'S LABOR'S LOST
978-1-935550-07-5

THE COMEDY OF ERRORS
978-1-935550-08-2

KING LEAR
978-1-935550-09-9

HENRY IV, PART 1
978-1-935550-11-2

OTHELLO
978-1-935550-10-5

All plays $7.95, available in bookstores everywhere

"Nick Newlin's 30-minute play cuttings are perfect for students who have no experience with Shakespeare. Each 30-minute mini-play is a play in itself with a beginning, middle, and end." —Michael Ellis-Tolaydo, Department of Theater, Film, and Media Studies, St Mary's College of Maryland

PHOTOCOPYING AND PERFORMANCE RIGHTS

No part of this publication may be reproduced or transmitted in any form, electronic, photocopying or otherwise, without the prior written permission of the publisher.

There is no royalty for performing *Much Ado About Nothing: The 30-Minute Shakespeare* in a classroom or on a stage; however, permission must be obtained for all playscripts used by the actors. The publisher hereby grants unlimited photocopy permission for one series of performances to all acting groups that have purchased at least five (5) copies of the paperback edition or one (1) copy of the downloadable PDF edition available for $12.95 from www.30MinuteShakespeare.com.